MUSIC WORKOUT

Grade 3

Jean Archibald   **Bernadette Marmion**

Royal Irish Academy of Music

GRADE 3

Syllabus

Note / Rest Values	Note values semibreve to semiquaver including quaver triplets. Rest values semibreve to semiquaver.
Time	Simple Duple $\frac{2}{4}$, $\frac{2}{2}$, ¢; Simple Triple $\frac{3}{4}$, $\frac{3}{2}$, $\frac{3}{8}$; Simple Quadruple $\frac{4}{4}$, $\frac{4}{2}$
Stave	Notes to two ledger lines above and below treble and bass staves. Transcribing from treble to bass and *vice versa* at the same pitch.
Scales and Intervals Major / Minor	Major scales, key signatures and tonic triads of keys up to two sharps and two flats. Intervals formed from the tonic of these major keys.
	Minor scales, key signatures and tonic triads of A, E and D. To be familar with the relevant tonic solfa names and understand the positioning of tones and semitones. (Harmonic or melodic form may be used at the candidate's choice.)
Composition	To compose the final two bars of a simple four-bar melody of which the opening two bars are given. The melody to be in the treble clef, keys of C, G or F, and in $\frac{2}{4}$ or $\frac{3}{4}$ time.
Observation	To answer simple questions about a melody appropriate to the grade.

A Note to the Teacher

The sight singing exercises are introduced by using Stick Notation ; this shows the solfa names and the rhythm. Hand signs are used as a visual aid to pitch. Reading from the stave is encouraged ; this is facilitated by the use of a ' *do* clef ' : ¢ . *do* may be pitched on any note to suit the student's range.

Text Signals

● indicates where new concepts and information are introduced.

■ indicates points to be memorised and useful hints.

First published in 1998 by
The Royal Irish Academy of Music
Westland Row, Dublin 2.

©1998 by The Royal Irish Academy of Music

ISBN 1 - 902140 - 04 - 4

Music processing Jean Archibald and Bernadette Marmion
Typesetting and graphics Creighton Music, Dublin 14.
Cover design Origin Design Associates.
Printed by: Colour World Print Ltd, Kilkenny

CONTENTS

1 | REVISION of KEYS : C G D and F MAJOR |

● Here are the key signatures and tonic triads of the scales you learned in Grades 1 and 2.

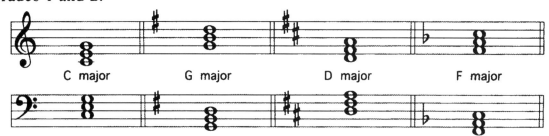

C major   G major   D major   F major

■ When required to write scales, always ask yourself these questions :

1. Clef : treble or bass?
2. Going up or down?   Going up and down?
3. With key signature? Without key signature (i.e. with accidentals)?
4. What note values (semibreves, minims, etc.)?
5. Are semitones to be marked?
6. Are solfa names required?

Exercise 1 Write tonic triads and scales as directed for the given keys. Mark semitones and give solfa names as required. Follow Exercise a) as a guide.

a) G major   Scale ascending, with key signature, in semibreves. Mark semitones. Give solfa names.

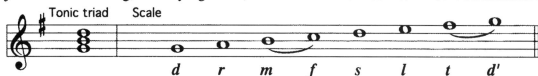

b) F major   Scale descending , without key signature, in minims. Mark semitones.

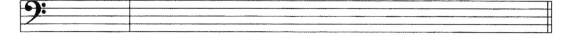

c) D major   Scale ascending, with key signature, in crotchets.

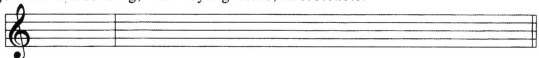

d) C major   Scale descending, in minims. Mark semitones. Give solfa names.

e) F major   Scale ascending, with key signature, in semibreves.

f) D major Scale descending, without key signature, in minims. Mark semitones

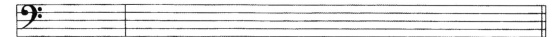

INTERVALS : 2nd, 3rd, 4th, 5th

● An **interval** is the ' distance ' between one sound and another. In other words, it is the difference in pitch between any two notes. The 'size' of an interval is measured by counting upwards the number of scale notes between the lower and upper note of the interval. When counting, both the upper and lower notes are included. For example :

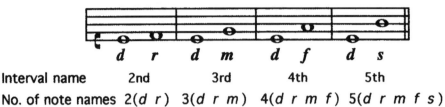

Interval name	2nd	3rd	4th	5th
No. of note names	2(*d r*)	3(*d r m*)	4(*d r m f*)	5(*d r m f s*)

Practise singing these intervals in solfa until you are sure of their sound.

The number name of an interval (2nd, 3rd, 4th, 5th) is its **numerical value**. Intervals also have other names, called **quality names**. In the intervals above, the 2nd and 3rd are called **Major 2nd** and **Major 3rd** but the 4th and 5th are called **Perfect 4th** and **Perfect 5th**. Later on you will learn more about why this is so.

Here are the four intervals you have sung. They are in the key of C major.

They are shown in the treble and bass clefs :

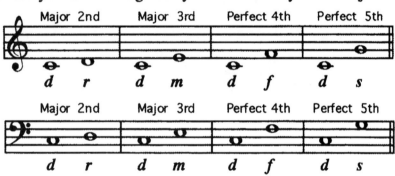

Exercise 2 Write the solfa names and interval names under the notes below. Check the clef and key signature each time. The first one is done as a guide.

INTERVALS in MELODIES

● An interval occurring in a melody is called a **melodic interval**. Actually, a melody is made up of a number of melodic intervals one after another. For the time being, we will measure only those intervals which have the tonic of their key as their lower note. It doesn't matter whether the lower note comes before or after the upper note - you still measure from the lower note.

Exercise 3 Name the key of each melody. Underneath each bracketed interval, write its name. (The same interval can occur more than once in a melody.)

Exercise 4 Add accidentals where needed, so that each melody is in the named key. Under each bracketed interval write the name of the interval.

MELODIC and HARMONIC INTERVALS

● If the two notes of an interval are sounded one after another, the interval is said to be **melodic** because this is the way the interval would sound if it were part of a melody or tune. Study the intervals on page 2 and you will see that they are all melodic intervals.

If the two notes of an interval are sounded at the same time, then the interval is part of a chord. A **chord** is a group of notes sounded together at the same time. Because harmony is concerned with chords, interval notes sounded at the same time are said to be **harmonic**. The following example shows the intervals in C major, written harmonically.

■ Notice how the Major 2nd is written. If you write the upper note exactly above the lower one, neither will be clear, so always write the upper note very close to, but not directly above, the lower note.

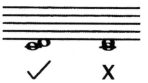

Exercise 5 Add another note beside or above the given note to make the intervals named below each stave. Check the clef and the key signature each time.

INTERVALS and TONIC TRIADS

A tonic triad is made up of the 1st, 3rd and 5th notes of a scale (*d, m, s*). If you sing these notes one after the other, you are singing melodically.

These notes can be sounded together to make a chord. Think of this as two separate intervals *d - m* (Maj.3rd) and *d - s* (Perfect 5th).

Maj. 3rd   Perf. 5th

Put them together and you get

Major Triad

The bottom note of any triad is called the **root**.
The middle note is called the **3rd** because it is a third higher than the root.
The top note is called the **5th** because it is a fifth higher than the root.
A **major triad** consists of a Major 3rd and a Perfect 5th.

INTERVALS and TRIADS without KEY SIGNATURES

Some exercises have asked you to write scales without key signatures, putting in whatever sharps or flats were needed as you went along. You can also write intervals and tonic triads without key signatures.This needs care.
For example, a Major 3rd above D is F♯, not F. Why ?
Because F♯ is the 3rd note in the <u>scale</u> of D major, and intervals are made up of <u>scale</u> notes.

If the interval is written with a key signature, nothing needs to be added to either note :

If the interval is written without a key signature,then the F♯ needs to be written in as an accidental :

The same is true of a tonic triad:

with key signature   without key signature

Exercise 6   Draw the following harmonic intervals without key signatures .

a)   Major 3rd   Perfect 5th   Perfect 4th   Major 2nd   Perfect 5th

b)   Perfect 4th   Major 3rd   Major 2nd   Perfect 5th   Major 3rd

c)   Major 2nd   Major 3rd   Perfect 4th   Major 2nd   Perfect 4th

Exercise 7   Draw the following tonic triads without key signatures.

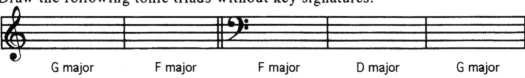

G major   F major   F major   D major   G major

SIGHT CLAPPING 1 : REVISION

● The table below shows the rhythm patterns used for clapping in Grade 2.

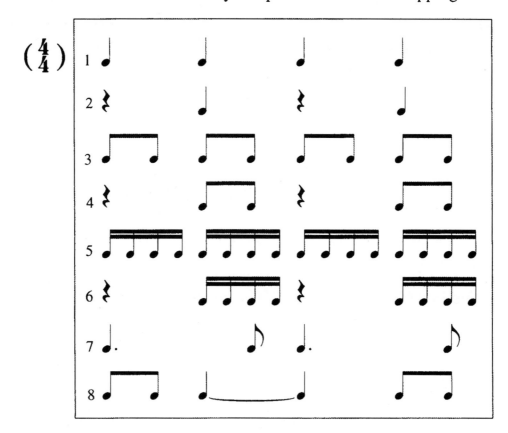

Exercise 8 Clap the rhythms shown in the table several times. Count aloud to help you keep a steady beat. Aim for a good rhythmic flow by accenting the first beat. Practise the patterns in many different orders.

Exercise 9 Clap each of the following rhythms while keeping a steady beat.

THE QUAVER TRIPLET

● When a composer wishes to break up a beat into 3 <u>equal</u> parts in $\frac{2}{4}$, $\frac{3}{4}$ or $\frac{4}{4}$ time, a **triplet** must be used. A triplet is shown by a figure 3 which may appear on its own or may be written with a slur or a bracket. A triplet slur looks like this : ⌒3⌒ . A triplet bracket looks like this: ⌐3⌐ . The following are quaver triplets:

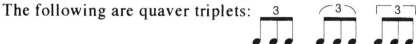

The notes of a triplet are played a little faster so that they fit into the time normally given to 2 of the same kind of note. For example :

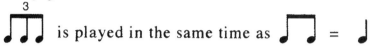

Exercise 10 Add the missing bar lines in each of the following extracts.

Sometimes two of the notes of a triplet are added together and written like this: ⌐3⌐ or like this: ⌐3⌐

■ Summary : i) A triplet group must always have three equal divisions.
      ii) Two of its notes may be added together in one longer note.

Exercise 11 Add the missing bar lines in the following extract.

Schumann Op. 82

Exercise 12 Draw circles to show how these notes make up crotchet beats. Then re-write, joining quavers and semiquavers where necessary. The beginning of the first exercise has been done as a guide.

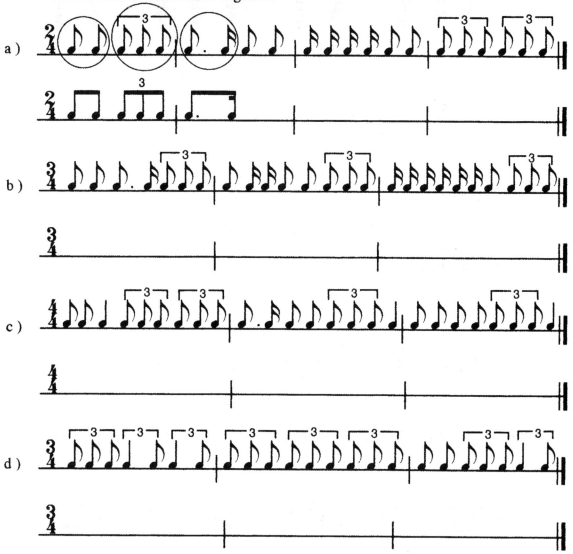

Exercise 13 Rewrite these melodies with the notes correctly grouped.

Schubert. "Winterreise"

Tchaikovsky. 'Sleigh Ride'

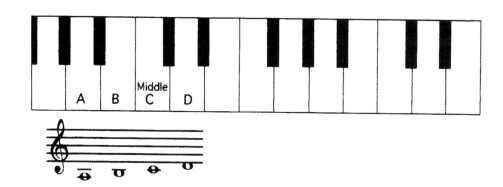

You already know D, C and B below the treble stave. Now A is added. It is on the 2nd ledger line <u>below</u> the stave.

■ When drawing notes in ledger lines and spaces, remember to keep the distance between the ledger lines the same as the distance between the stave lines.

Exercise 14 Practise drawing treble notes in ledger lines and spaces by copying these notes into the blank bars.

Exercise 15 Draw two notes with the same name but at different pitches. One of the notes will be a ledger line or space above or below the stave (except for F).

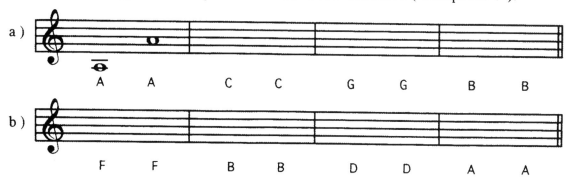

● Do you remember the notes you learned to sing in previous grades ? In Grade 2 you learnt to sing *d r m f s* and *l*. Tunes were written in stick notation and on the stave using C to show the position of *do* . Melodies were also included in the keys of C, G, D and F. You learned hand signs for the solfa names and sometimes finished a tune by composing your own 'missing bar '.The exercises below will help to revise these points.

On page 62 the hand signs are listed for you to revise them if necessary.

Exercise 16 Sing each of these tunes using tonic solfa names. As you sing, tap a quiet steady beat with your hand or foot, or make hand signs.

In the next melody one bar has been left out. Sing the part of the melody which is given. Then compose your own missing bar, writing in the notes and the rhythm. When you have done this, sing the whole tune.

SINGING with SOLFA 2 : ADDING LOW S,

● So far you have sung tunes in which all the notes were above *do*. In the next group of exercises the <u>low</u> *so* is added. In stick notation a small tick is written like this : *s,* . This shows that it is <u>below</u> *do*.

Exercise 17 These are some singing drills to help you learn the new sound *s,* . Tap a steady beat as you sing.

Exercise 18 Sing these tunes with solfa names. Keep a steady beat.

This is part of a minuet by Haydn. Study the music carefully. Then answer the questions below.

1. Explain the meaning of these musical terms and signs :

Moderato _____ (above staves) _____

♩=120 _____ 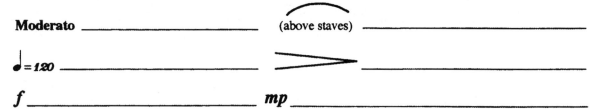 _____

f _____ mp _____

2 a) Name the key in which the music is written. _____

   b) Find three notes beside one another which make up the tonic triad. Draw a large circle around all three notes.

   c) Explain the group of three notes at the end of bar 1. _____

   _____

   d) Is ¾ time described as duple, triple or quadruple ? _____

   e) Draw an X above two notes which are tied.

   f) For how many beats does this tied sound last ? _____

3. a) Give the letter name of the note marked * (bar 2). _____

   b) Draw a box around the lowest note. What is its letter name ? _____

   c) Name the interval between the first two notes of the melody. _____

   d) The first 4 bars are repeated later. Where does the repeat begin ? Bar _____

   e) The last 3 bars are part of a scale. Write the solfa name below each note in these bars.

13

Q. 1 (a) Write the scale belonging to the given key signature. Write the scale going up in minims. Include the solfa names and mark the semitones.

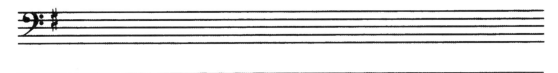

(b) Add sharps (as accidentals) to any notes which need them to make the scale of D major. Add solfa names and mark the semitones.

Q. 2 Write the key signatures and tonic triads for each of these keys.

G major   F major   D major   G major

Q. 3 (a) Describe each interval . The first one is already done as a guide.

Major 3rd   _____   _____   _____

(b) Draw another note after each of the given notes to make these melodic intervals.

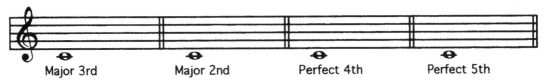

Major 3rd   Major 2nd   Perfect 4th   Perfect 5th

Q. 4 Add bar lines to the following melody.

Schubert "Standchen"

Q. 5 (a) Draw circles to show how these notes make up crotchet beats.

(b) Re-write the notes correctly grouped.

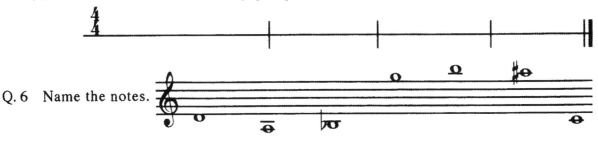

Q. 6 Name the notes.

_____   _____   _____   _____   _____

13

● Do you remember the pattern of tone and semitone steps which form a major scale?

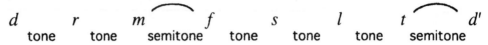

Now use this keyboard drawing to pick out a major scale starting on B♭.

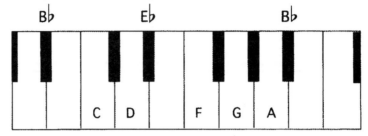

E♭ is needed to put the semitone step in the correct place.

This is the scale of B♭ major ascending and descending. It is written with accidentals, Notice that you need a ♭ for the last note as well as for the first. Solfa names and semitone marks are added.

On the treble stave this scale can also be written one octave lower.

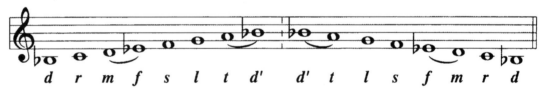

This is the scale of B♭ major with its flats written as a key signature. The B♭ is written only once in the key signature - the one B♭ stands for both the first and last scale notes. The flats of the key signature are always written like this, whether or not the scale begins on a high or low B♭.

Exercise 19 a) Write the scale of B♭ major ascending on the bass stave. Use accidentals.

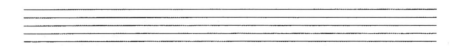

b) Add a clef and key signature to make this the scale of B flat major.

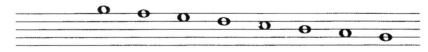

● The scales and keys you have learnt so far are C, G, D, F and B♭. Why did we start scales on these particular notes ? This is the reason :

The major scales are divided into two groups - those with sharps and those with flats.

The scale of C C has no sharps or flats. But it is very important as it is used as a starting point by each scale group.

The sharp scales Each new sharp scale starts on the 5th note of the scale before it.

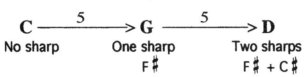

C ——5——> G ——5——> D
No sharp   One sharp   Two sharps
            F♯   F♯ + C♯

So the keynote or tonic of each new sharp scale is a Perfect 5th above the keynote of the scale before it. Notice that the keynote is one step higher than the last sharpened note.(G is a step above F♯, D is a step above C♯.)

The flat scales Each new flat scale starts on the 4th note of the scale before it.

C ——4——> F ——4——> B♭
No flat   One flat   Two flats
           B♭   B♭ + E♭

So the keynote (tonic) of each new flat scale is a Perfect 4th above the keynote of the scale before it. Notice that the keynote is 4 notes lower than the last flattened note.(B♭ is 4 notes lower than E♭.)

Exercise 20 Draw tonic triads to match these key signatures.

Exercise 21 Add clefs and accidentals to make the triads match the names underneath.

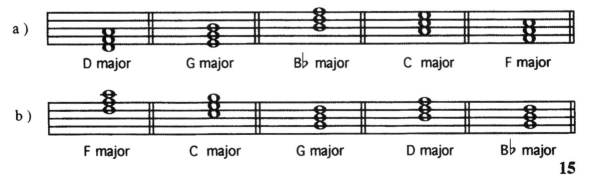

● Revise the intervals introduced on page 2. Here they are again but with three new ones added.

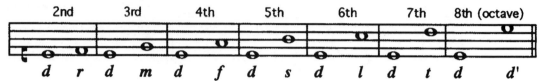

Practise singing all the intervals in solfa until you are sure of their sound.

The new intervals are made by using the tonic (*d*) and the 6th (*l*), 7th (*t*) or 8th (*d'*) notes of the major scale.

The quality names for these intervals are : 6th - Major
                                              7th - Major
                                              8th - Perfect

This is the full range of intervals in the key of C major:

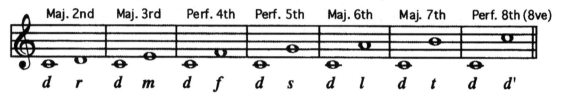

The names of these intervals are the same for every major key.

■ | Learn this sequence : Major, Major, Perfect, Perfect, Major, Major, Perfect |

Exercise 22 Name the key and the interval in each bar.

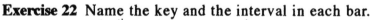

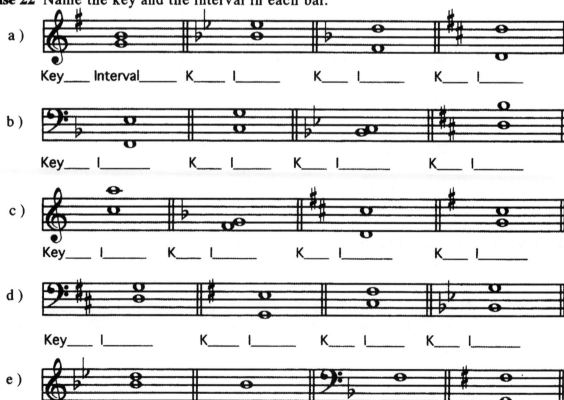

Exercise 23 These melodies are written with accidentals instead of key signatures.
(i) Name the key of each. ii) Under each bracketed interval write its name.

Exercise 24 Each note in this exercise is the tonic of a key. Using accidentals instead of key signatures, add one note above or after the given note to form the intervals.

Exercise 25 (i) Name the key to which each of these tonic triads belongs. (ii) Re-write the triads on the stave below, using key signatures instead of accidentals.

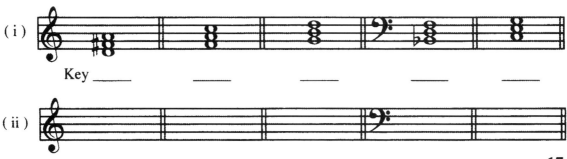

● This group of clapping exercises introduces  and combines it with patterns already learnt.

Exercise 26 Clap these patterns alternately or as a duet with another person.

Exercise 27 Clap the following rhythms, always counting an even beat.

a)

b)

c)

d)

e)

f)

g)

h)

i)

$\frac{2}{2}$: ¢

In $\frac{2}{4}$, $\frac{3}{4}$ and $\frac{4}{4}$ times the beats are crotchet beats. Sometimes a composer may choose to write his music using minim beats or even quaver beats. This does not actually change the sound but the music will look different when written down.

The alternative name for a minim is a half note, so a time signature with 2 minim beats in a bar is shown by $\frac{2}{2}$ or ¢. Of all the time signatures using minim beats, $\frac{2}{2}$ is the one you will meet most frequently.

Study the following rhythm patterns :

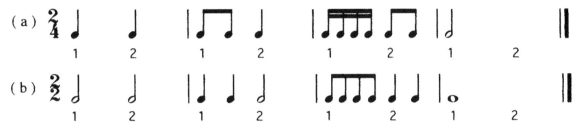

Both of these rhythms sound exactly the same. But they look different because (a) is written using crotchet beats; (b) is written using minim beats.

Another way to say this : in (a) the counts (beats) are measured in crotchets, while in (b) the counts (beats) are measured in minims.

Both $\frac{2}{4}$ and $\frac{2}{2}$ are described as **simple duple** times.

Exercise 28 Draw the bar lines in each of the following.

THE SEMIQUAVER REST

1. A semiquaver rest is written like this :

2. When a semiquaver rest occurs within a beat, the other notes may be joined around it. For example :

3. A semiquaver is $\frac{1}{4}$ of a crotchet beat. When adding rests, build up the beat in easy stages, i.e. always put the two quarters together to make up a half, then add the other half to finish the beat.

For example :

Exercise 29 Add the missing bar lines in each of the following.

Exercise 30 Add one rest at each place marked * to make the bar complete.

Exercise 31 Add the missing rest or rests at * . Take care with the grouping.

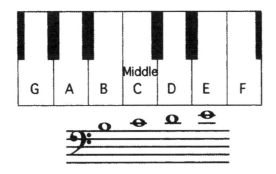

You already know B, C and D above the bass stave. Now E is added. It is on the 2nd ledger line above the stave.

Exercise 32 Practise drawing bass notes in the ledger lines and spaces by copying these notes into the blank bars.

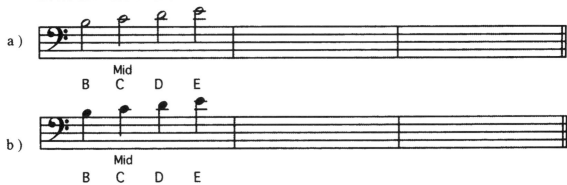

The treble and bass staves are separated by only one line - the Middle C line. In the diagram below, it is shown as a broken line because it is always used as a ledger line.

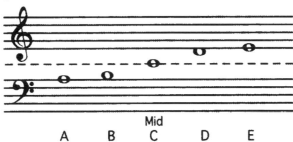

From the next diagram you can see how A, B, Middle C, D and E can be written in two different ways, either below the treble or above the bass. They sound the same whichever way you write them.

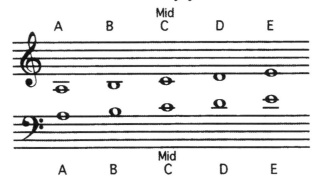

EXERCISES on LEDGER LINES and SPACES

Exercise 33 Write the letter name below each note.

Exercise 34 Draw two notes with the same letter name but at different pitches. One of the notes is to be <u>on</u> the stave, the other is to be a ledger line or space <u>above</u> or <u>below</u> the stave). The first one is done as a guide.

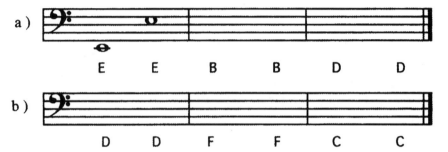

a)

    E   E   B   B   D   D

b)

    D   D   F   F   C   C

Exercise 35 Add a clef in front of each note so that its letter name is correct.

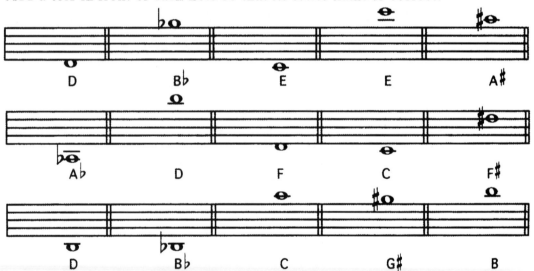

D   B♭   E   E   A♯

A♭   D   F   C   F♯

D   B♭   C   G♯   B

Exercise 36 All the notes in this exercise are in the middle of the keyboard. Write letter names under all the notes. Then re-write each note at the same pitch (i.e. the same sound) but using the other clef. The first one is done as a guide.

C   C

Exercise 37 Sing each tune with solfa names. Tap a steady beat or make hand signs as you sing.

Exercise 38 In the next melodies one bar has been left out. Sing the part of the melody which is given. Then compose your own missing bar, writing in the notes and the rhythm. When you have done this, sing the whole tune.

GENERAL OBSERVATION 2

This is part of a piano sonata by Mozart. Study the music. Then answer the questions below.

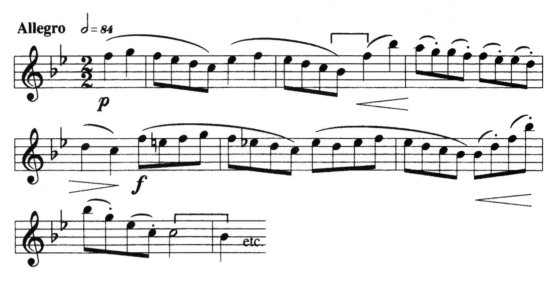

1. Explain the meaning of these musical terms and signs:

    p_____ **Allegro** _____

    ♩= *84* _____ > _____

    f _____ < _____

2. Fill in the blanks to complete each sentence.

    The music is written in the key of ___ major. The time signature shows that

    there are ___ beats in a bar and each beat is worth a _____ .The melody

    begins on *so* and ends on _____ . The letter name of the highest note is ____

    The pattern of the first six notes is repeated, but one step _____ .There

    is an accidental in bar ____; the letter name of the note is _____ .

3. a) Is ²₂ time duple, triple or quadruple? _____

    b) Show another way of writing this time signature. _____

    c) Draw a large circle around 3 notes beside each other which form the tonic triad.

    d) Name the interval marked ⌐─⌐ in bar 2. _____

    e) Name the interval marked ⌐─⌐ at the end. _____

Q. 1 Add a clef and accidentals to these notes to make the scale of B flat major.

Q. 2 Write the tonic triads for the keys named. Use accidentals instead of a key signature.

G major   D major   B flat major   F major

Q. 3 Write the solfa names and interval names under each pair of notes in D major.

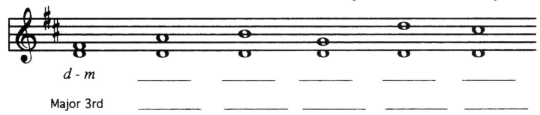

d - m   _____ _____ _____ _____ _____

Major 3rd   _____ _____ _____ _____ _____

Q.4 Add a note above each of the given notes to make the intervals named in B♭ major. Use accidentals instead of a key signature.

Major 3rd   Perfect 4th   Perfect 5th   Major 7th   Major 6th   Perfect 8ve

Q. 5 Give the letter name of each note. Then draw another note with the same letter name but one octave higher.

_____ _____ _____ _____ _____

Q. 6 a) Draw bar lines in the following melody.

Purcell

b) Show another way of writing the time signature ₵ _____

c) Below is the same tune written in two ways. Add the missing top number to complete each time signature.

i) ... ii) ...

d) Which of the above tunes is counted in minims ? _____

Q. 7 Add the missing rest or rests at the places marked * .

Mozart

All the scales you have learnt so far are called major scales. Now you are going to learn a new scale with a new sound - the **minor** scale. There are 3 kinds of minor scale: natural minor, harmonic minor and melodic minor. The first one you will learn about is the **natural minor scale**.

You remember how the scale of C major was played on the keyboard.

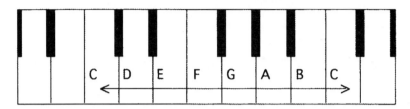

Here it is with solfa names underneath and the semitones marked. These are between notes 3 - 4 and 7 - 8 going up; 8 -7 and 4 - 3 coming down.

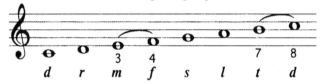

Imagine that instead of starting the scale on C, you start 2 notes lower on A. But you still use only white keys, as you do with the scale of C.

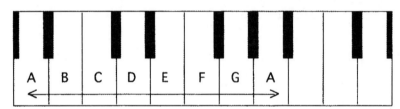

C is still your *do*, so by moving down 2 notes you are now starting the scale on *la* (*la* below *do*). Like the major scale, the minor scale has 8 notes, so if you begin on *la*, you end on *la*.

The semitones still come between *t - d* and *m - f* as they did in the major scale, but the numbering of the notes making the semitones has changed. These are 2 -3 and 5 - 6 going up; 6 - 5 and 3 - 2 going down.

The natural minor scale written above would fit more comfortably onto the treble stave if it were an 8ve higher.

The **tonic** is the **first** note of a scale, so *la* is the tonic of this minor scale.

THE HARMONIC MINOR SCALE

Many tunes are written using the notes of the minor scale. Most of these tunes end with the 7th note of the scale going to the tonic.

m d' d' t t d' d' l m m s s l

Try singing this tune.

Now sing it again raising *so* a semitone. This time the tune will sound <u>more finished</u>. When *so* is raised a semitone, it is given the name *si* .

m d' d' t t d' d' l m m si si l

Sing both versions of the tune a few times to appreciate their difference. If we write out the natural minor scale again, but change *so* to *si* , we get this:

| | 2 | 3 | | 5 | 6 | 7 | 8 | 7 | 6 | 5 | | 3 | 2 | |
| l | t | d | r | m | f | si | l | si | f | m | r | d | t | l |

This scale is called the **harmonic minor scale**.

Play it on the keyboard. It is exactly the same going up as coming down.

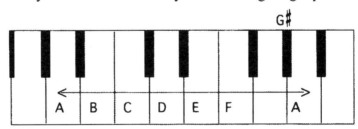

Did you notice there are <u>three</u> semitones? These are *t - d* and *m - f* as before, but because *so* becomes *si*, there is now an extra semitone *si - l*. The numbering of the notes making the semitones is now :
2 - 3 , 5 - 6 , 7 - 8 going up ; 8 - 7 , 6 - 5 , 3 - 2 coming down.

Exercise 39 Write the harmonic minor scale of A as required above each stave. Mark the semitones and add solfa names to each scale.

a) Bass clef, ascending and descending in semibreves.

b) Treble clef, descending in minims.   c) Bass clef, ascending in minims.

Melodies which are written using the notes of a major scale are said to be **'in a major key '**. Melodies written using the notes of a minor scale are said to be **'in a minor key '**.

If a tune is in a minor key, it does not matter which kind of minor scale notes are being used: natural, harmonic or melodic. Many folksongs, for instance, use the natural minor scale. Other songs and instrumental pieces use the harmonic or melodic scales, or a mixture of both. The important thing is to be able to recognise whether a melody is in a <u>major key</u> or a <u>minor key</u>.

There are two main clues to help you decide if a tune is in a minor key.
    1 The tune ends on *la*, the tonic of the minor scale.
    2 There is an accidental in the tune for the 7th note of the scale.(But remember that it can happen that a particular tune may not include the 7th note of the scale.)

Compare these two melodies.

Example (i)

Key : C major

Example (ii)

Key : A minor

Exercise 40 State whether each of these tunes is in the key of C major or A minor.

"Wareham"

Key : _____

Mozart: Symphony No.40

Key : _____

Grieg: Peer Gynt -"Anitra's Dance"

Key : _____

Beethoven: Symphony No.5

Key : _____

●   This group of clapping exercises introduces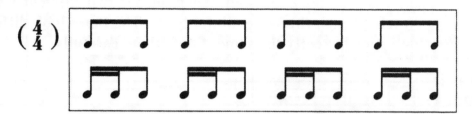

Exercise 41 Clap these patterns alternately or as a duet.

Exercise 42 Clap the following rhythms while counting a steady beat.

a)

b)

c)

d)

e)

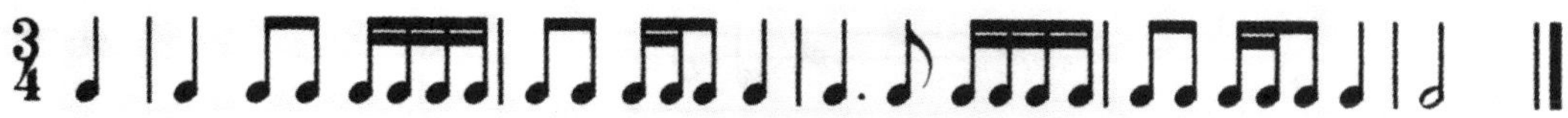

f)

g)

h)

i)

On page 19 you learned how a composer could choose to write his music using either crotchet beats or minim beats. Read page 19 again to revise the points made there.

This is a tune you probably know well. It is printed in two different ways : (a) using crotchet beats; (b) using minim beats. The tunes <u>look</u> different but they both <u>sound</u> exactly the same. Study them carefully.

$\frac{3}{4}$ and $\frac{3}{2}$ are both described as **simple triple** time.

Exercise 43 Add the missing bar lines in each of these extracts.

Exercise 44 The composer wrote the following piece using minim beats. Re-write the melody to show how it would appear in $\frac{3}{4}$ using crotchet beats.

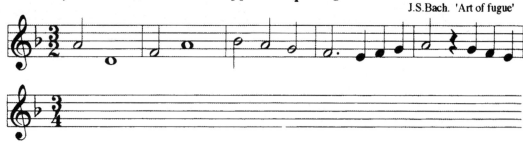

The minim is the beat unit in $\frac{2}{2}$ and $\frac{3}{2}$ times. To help with the reading of the rhythm, shorter notes are grouped (beamed) into minim beats.

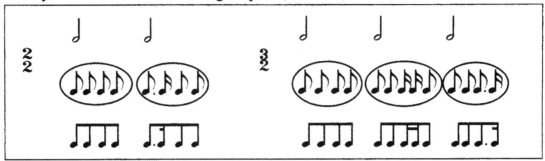

The grouping of rests also follows the same principle as before, i.e.

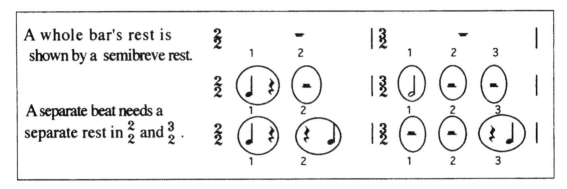

A whole bar's rest is shown by a semibreve rest.

A separate beat needs a separate rest in $\frac{2}{2}$ and $\frac{3}{2}$.

Exercise 45 Circle notes to show how they make up minim beats. Re-write, joining quavers and semiquavers where necessary. The start of exercise (a) is done as a guide.

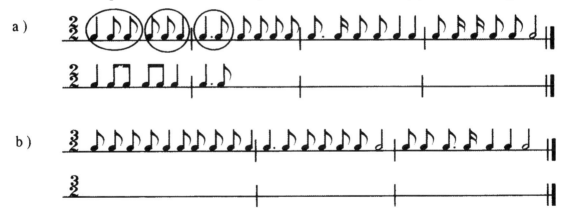

Exercise 46 Add missing rest or rests at * . Take care with grouping.

J.S. Bach: Organ Prelude

Beethoven: Pf. Sonata Op.13.

• On page 21 you learned how the notes in the middle of the keyboard can be written on the treble or on the bass staves using ledger lines. Here they are again.

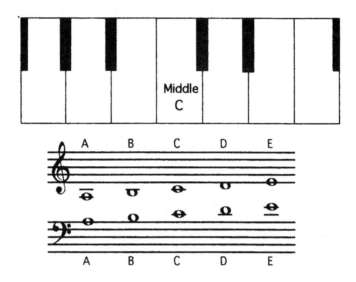

Exercise 47 In the exercises which follow, you will be asked to write out tunes using a different clef but at the same pitch. In other words, the clefs will be different but the sound will be the same. The first two exercises have been begun for you. All the tunes are in the key of A minor.

SINGING with SOLFA 4 : *s, d r m f s*

Exercise 48 Sing each tune using solfa names. Tap a steady beat or make hand signs as you sing.

Exercise 49 Each melody omits the last 2 bars. Sing the given part. Decide the notes and rhythm which sound best in the missing bars. Complete the tune, then sing it.

This is the opening of the right hand part of a piece written for keyboard. Study the music. Then answer the questions below.

J.S.Bach

1.   Add terms and signs to the music to show the following :

   a) The piece is to be played quickly and lively; the metronome speed is 112 crotchets per minute.

   b) Bar 1 is moderately loud.

   c) The notes in bars 2 and 4 are to be played smoothly.

   d) The crotchets in bars 5 and 6 are to be short and detached.

   e) Bar 7 gets gradually louder.

2.a) Is the music written in C major or A minor ?   _____

   b) Can you find a part of the melody where the first 5 notes of the scale follow one another? Draw a bracket ⌐‾‾‾‾¬ over these notes.

   c) Write the solfa names below the notes in bar 1.

   d) Draw the missing rest at X in bar 7.

   e) What is the time name for this rest ?   _____

3. Tick the box to show whether the following sentences are ' true ' or ' false '.

   a) Bar 1 is repeated exactly in bar 3.   `true` `false`

   b) The shape of bar 1 is used again in bar 3 but one step higher.   `true` `false`

   c) Bar 4 has the same rhythm as bar 2.   `true` `false`

   d) Bar 5 is repeated an octave lower in bar 6.   `true` `false`

   e) Bar 5 is repeated a 3rd lower in bar 6.   `true` `false`

TEST 3

Q. 1 Add the bar lines in the following melody.

Q 2 Add a rest or rests at each place marked * to make the bars complete.

Beethoven: Bagatelle Op. 33

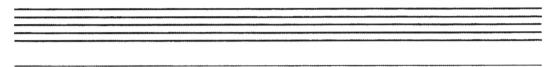

Q. 3 Write the scale of A minor (harmonic) going up and down in the bass clef. Include the solfa names and mark the semitones.

Q. 4 Write the named intervals without key signature in D major. Make harmonic intervals by writing a note above the given note in each case.

    Perfect 5th   Major 7th   Perfect 8ve   Major 3rd   Major 2nd   Perfect 4th

Q. 5 Is the following melody written in C major or A minor ?

Key_____

Q. 6 Write the solfa names below each note of the following melody in G major. Sing through the melody and compose the final bar.

Q. 7 Notes in the middle of the keyboard can be written 2 ways - below the treble or above the bass. In the following question draw lines to link notes which sound the same.

Q. 8 Add the time signature to the following piece.

J.S. Bach: Chorale Prelude

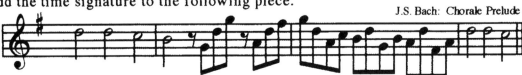

35

E MINOR SCALE

●   The scale of G major is written below the keyboard drawing.

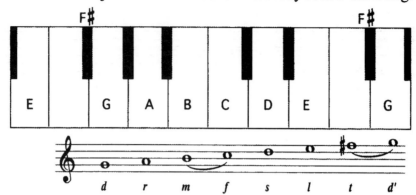

Now make a natural minor scale, by starting on *la* instead of *do*.

To turn the natural minor scale into a harmonic minor scale, another semitone is needed between the last two notes. (If you are not sure about this, refer to page 27, revising the harmonic minor scale starting on A.)
To obtain the third semitone (*si - l*) the 7th note must be raised with an accidental, in this case a ♯ .

Excercise 50   Write the harmonic minor scale of E in the way indicated above each stave. Mark the semitones and add the solfa names below each scale.

a) Bass clef, ascending and descending in semibreves.

b) Treble clef, descending in minims.

c) Bass clef, ascending in minims.

d) Treble clef, ascending in crotchets.

RELATIVE MAJORS and MINORS

● Compare the scale of C major and the natural minor scale of A.

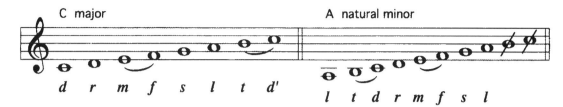

You can see that, although they <u>start</u> on different notes, the notes used in the scales are the same. This becomes very clear when you play the two scales on a keyboard because you are only using <u>white</u> keys.

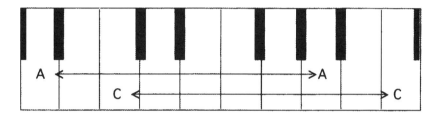

The fact that both scales use basically the same notes means that they are related. Think of the two scales as cousins !

> A minor is said to be the relative minor of C major.
> C major is said to be the relative major of A minor.

● Even when the harmonic form of the minor scale is used, it is still the relative minor of C major.

Now take another pair of scales: G major and E minor.

E minor uses basically the same notes as G major, so it is the relative minor of G.

Here is G major again, with E minor in its harmonic form.

● Apart from D and D♯, the notes in both scales are the same. Therefore

> E minor is the relative minor of G major.
> G major is the relative major of E minor.

● This is the scale of G major written in two different ways: first with F♯ as an accidental, then with F♯ as a key signature.

This is E minor, the relative minor of G major, written in two different ways. The harmonic minor form of the scale is used.

In the first example, both F♯ and D♯ are written as accidentals. In the second, F♯ is written as a key signature and D♯ as an accidental.

● Because G major and E minor are ' related ', they use the same key signature. Think of the key signature as rather like a surname. If your surname is Mozart, you probably have a cousin whose surname is also Mozart.

> Music written in a minor key uses the key signature of its relative major.

> The accidental used to raise the 7th note of a minor scale is <u>always</u> an accidental - it can <u>never</u> be part of a key signature.

Exercise 51 Here are some minor scales to write. In the E minor ones, if you are asked to write without key signature, remember to put in the F♯ as an accidental. The 7th note should be raised in all cases. Mark the semitones. Add solfa names.

a)Harmonic minor scale. Begin on A ; ascend in crotchets. Use an accidental.

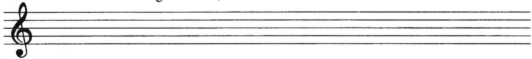

b) Harmonic minor scale. Begin on E; ascend in semibreves. Use a key signature and an accidental.

c) Harmonic minor scale. Begin on E; ascend and descend in minims.Use accidentals.

d) Harmonic minor scale. Begin on A; ascend and descend in minims. Use accidentals.

● The next group of clapping exercises combines  and

Exercise 52 Clap these rhythm patterns alternately or as a round.

Exercise 53 Clap the following rhythms while counting a steady beat.

● You have already learned about $\frac{2}{2}$ and $\frac{3}{2}$ times. Another time using minim beats is $\frac{4}{2}$ time. In $\frac{4}{2}$ time there are 4 minim beats in a bar, and for this reason it is described as **simple quadruple** time. Nowadays $\frac{4}{2}$ is little used, but you often come across it in older music and in church music.

Exercise 54 Add bar lines to the following pieces in $\frac{4}{2}$ time.

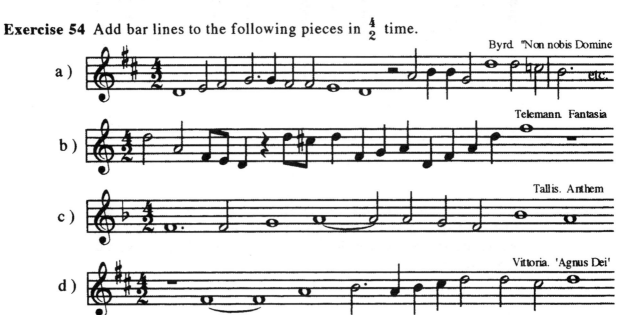

Exercise 55 Add the time signature to each of the following. In some cases, where one number of the time signature has been included, add the other number.

LEDGER LINES and SPACES above THE TREBLE

● You already know some of the ledger lines and spaces below and above the treble stave. Now one more note is added above - C. This is written on the second ledger line above the stave.

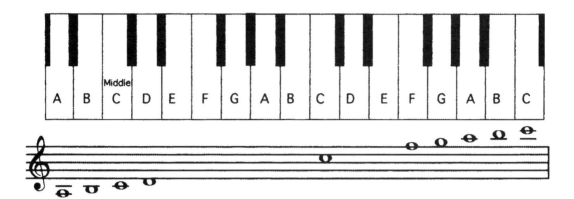

Exercise 56 Fill in the notes which are missing in these tunes, writing them on ledger lines and spaces above the treble stave. Use the note values shown.
Put accidentals on the same level as the notes they belong to; avoid unnecessary repetition of accidentals.

Handel. "Music for the Royal Fireworks"

Haydn. Oxford Symphony

Chopin. Mazurka No.15

Mozart 'Eine Kleine Nachtmusik'

41

THE SCALE of D MINOR

The scale of F major is written below the keyboard drawing.

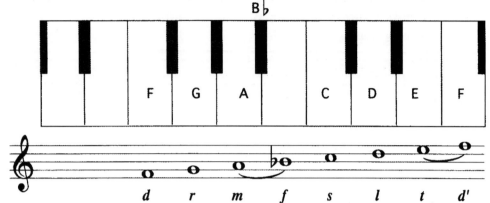

Now we will make a natural minor scale by beginning and finishing on *la* instead of *do*.

To turn the natural minor scale of D into a harmonic minor scale, a third semitone between the last two notes is needed.(Revise the harmonic minor scale beginning on A. If you are not sure about this, see page 27.) To obtain this third semitone (*si - l*) we have to raise the seventh note of the scale with an accidental - in this case a ♯ .

Exercise 57 Write the harmonic minor scale of D on the staves in the ways indicated. Use accidentals. Mark the semitones and add the solfa names.

a) Bass clef, ascending and descending in semibreves.

b) Treble clef, ascending and descending in minims.

c) Bass clef, ascending in minims.   d) Treble clef, ascending in crotchets.

EXERCISES on MINOR SCALES

Exercise 58 Add the correct clef, key signature and accidental to each scale to make the harmonic minor scale named.

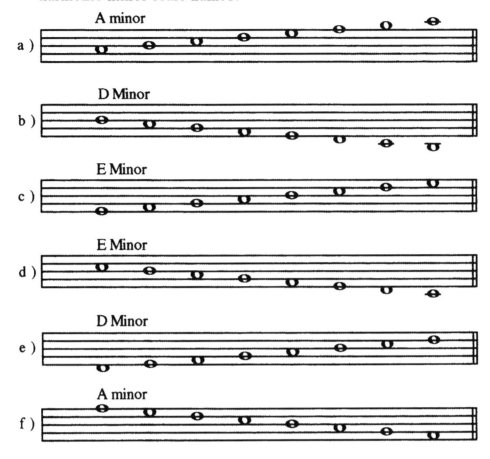

Exercise 59 Write the following scales. Do not use key signatures.

a) A minor. Treble clef, ascending and descending in minims.

b) E minor. Bass clef, ascending in crotchets.

c) D minor. Treble clef, descending in crotchets.

d) E minor. Bass clef, ascending and descending in minims.

In these tunes *ti* (*t*) and high *do* (*d'*) are added to complete the major scale. *ti* is a step (tone) above *la* and a half step (semitone) below high *do*.

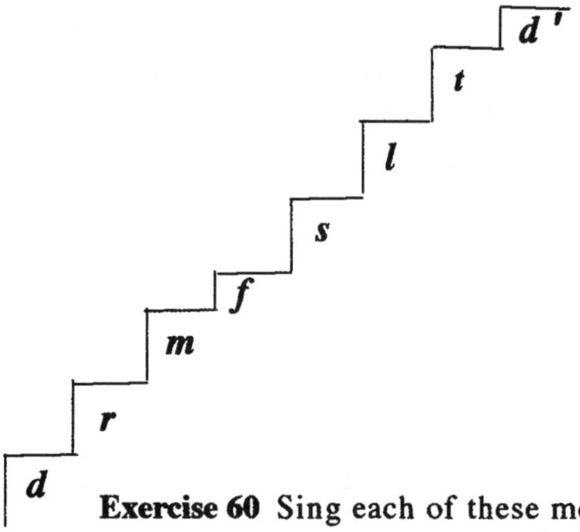

The hand sign for *ti* is

Exercise 60 Sing each of these melodies using tonic solfa names. While singing either tap a steady beat or make the hand signs.

a) 4/4 | d r m f | s l s | s l t d' | t t d' ||

b) 3/4 | d r m | r m f | s l t | d'. ||

c) 4/4 | d m s f | m r d | d m s s | l t d' ||

d) 2/4 | d m | s d' | s l | s | s l | t d' | t t | d' ||

e) [staff notation] d ... d'

f) [staff notation] d ... d'

g) [staff notation] d ... d'

h) [staff notation] d ... d'

SINGING with SOLFA 6 : COMPLETING MELODIES

■ When completing a melody, it is important to sing the tune a few times
so that you can hear which notes and rhythm sound best in the final bars.
Most melodies will sound more complete when ending on a long *do*.
You may find it easier to jot down your ideas using stick notation first,
before writing them on the stave. Always sing the completed melody.

Exercise 61 Finish each melody by composing another two bars.

GENERAL OBSERVATION 4

This is part of a minuet by Haydn. Study the music carefully, then answer the questions below.

1. Explain these terms and signs.

Andante _____   *dimin. e ritard.* _____

mf _____   **a tempo** _____

⌢ _____   ♩ = *108* _____

2. a) Name the <u>major</u> key in which the music is written. ——————

   b) Find three notes beside one another which make up the tonic triad. Draw a large circle around all three notes.

   c) All the groups of quavers have a 3 written above or below them . What does this mean?

   _____

   d) Put an X above any chromatic note, i.e. a note which does not belong to the key.

3. a) Study bars 5, 6 and 7. Apart from the same rhythm pattern, what other connection is there between these three bars? _____

   b) Give the letter names of notes in bar 5 marked: u ___ , v ___ ; in bar 7: x ___ , y ___ , z ___

   c) Name the interval between the last two notes in bar 1. _____

   d) $\frac{3}{4}$ means three crotchet beats in each bar. What would the time signature be, if the beats were minim beats ? _____

TEST 4

Q. 1 Name each note. Using ledger lines or spaces above and below the stave, write 2 notes with the same letter name, one octave higher and one octave lower than the given note.

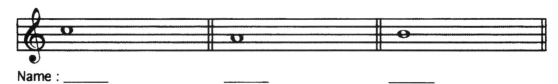

Name : _____   _____   _____

Q. 2 Add the missing rest or rests where you see * . Take care with grouping.

Q. 3 a) Fill in the blanks to complete each sentence.

   i) G major and ___ minor are related. ii) F major and ____ minor are related.

   iii) When major and minor scales are related, they share the same ____ signature.

   b) Add the clef, key signature and accidentals to make the scale of E harmonic minor. Mark the semitones and add the solfa names.

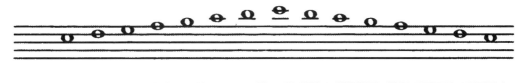

_____   _____

Q. 4 a) Sing these two bars using solfa names and keeping a steady beat. Then compose two bars to finish the tune. Sing the whole tune when you have finished writing.

   b) Now write the completed tune in the key of G major.

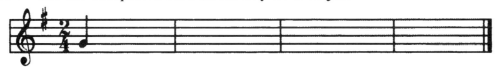

Q. 5 Add the time signature to the following piece.

Q. 6 Answer the questions about the following melody.

   a) Is the music in the key of F major or D minor? _____

   b) Is the time signature measuring the beats in crotchets or minims? _____

   c) Is the time described as duple, triple or quadruple? _____

REVISION EXERCISES on MAJOR KEYS and INTERVALS

Go back to pages 2 and 16 and revise what you learned about intervals. Then do the exercises below.

Exercise 62 Identify these intervals. In each, the lower note is the tonic of a major key.

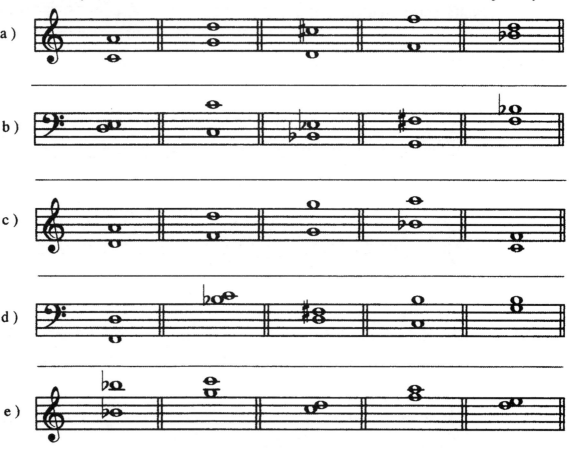

Exercise 63 Draw another note above each of the given notes to make intervals in the named keys. Do **not** use key signatures.

MINOR KEYS and TONIC TRIADS : EXERCISES

As with major keys, minor keys also have tonic triads, made from the 1st, 3rd and 5th notes of the scale. In the major key, the solfa notes used in the tonic triad are *d m s*. In the minor key, the solfa notes used are *l d m*.

Exercise 64 Identify the keys of these melodies. All are in minor keys. Some are with key signatures, others without. After each, name the key and write the tonic triad.

This is the natural minor scale beginning on A, ascending and descending, Note the semitones. If necessary, refer to page 26 to revise it.

l   t   d   r   m   f   s   l   s   f   m   r   d   t   l

This scale becomes the harmonic minor scale by raising the 7th note, going up and down. (See page 27, if necessary.)

l   t   d   r   m   f   si   l   si   f   m   r   d   t   l

When you play this scale on the keyboard, notice a large step marked ⌐‾⌐ between the 6th and 7th notes, i.e. between F and G♯. This step is 3 semitones wide, whereas all the other steps in the scale are tones or semitones. This larger step is not difficult to <u>play</u>, but it is a little awkward to <u>sing</u>. One way to 'smooth ' the interval is to raise the 6th note as well as the 7th. This makes a step of a tone between the 6th and 7th notes and is easier to sing.

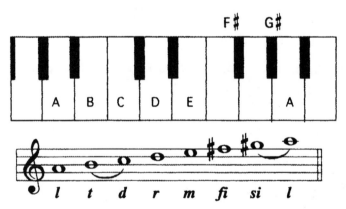

l   t   d   r   m   fi   si   l

But now there is another problem. If you play this new scale going up, you hear and see that the upper part sounds like a major scale. To remind us that the scale is a minor one, we use the natural minor scale to descend.

 2 3 7 8 6 5 3 2

l   t   d   r   m   fi   si   l   l   so   fa   m   r   d   t   l

This is called the **melodic minor scale**. It is given this name because it is mainly used in <u>writing melodies</u>.

The other type of minor scale, **the harmonic minor scale**, is used mainly for <u>intervals and chords</u> which are the basis of 'harmony' in music.

MELODIC MINORS and KEY SIGNATURES

● These are the harmonic minor and melodic minor scales in the other two keys you have learned - E minor and D minor.

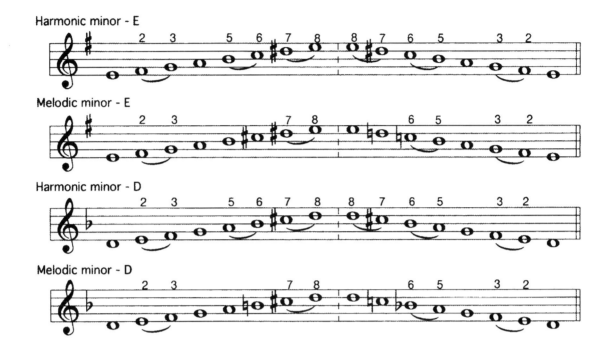

■ Notice the following points :

1 Key signatures : the harmonic and melodic minors are just different versions of the same scale. They are like two brothers or sisters. They have the same key signature - the key signature of their relative major. (E minor is related to G major; D minor is related to F major.)

2 Look at the position of the semitones and see how many there are.

3 In D melodic minor ascending, the 6th note (B♭)is raised by a ♮ . The flat is restored descending.

Exercise 65 Write these three melodic minor scales ascending and descending as above, using the bass clef. Mark the semitones.

Exercise 66 Use the table to combine in practice all the clapping patterns in this grade. When clapping the patterns, vary the order in many different ways.

Exercise 67 Organise one or two people to clap the patterns in the table above with you as a round.

Exercise 68 These are some more rhythms for you to clap. Always keep a steady beat.

TIME SIGNATURES : Adding $\frac{3}{8}$

● You have already learnt how music may be written down using crotchet beats, as in $\frac{2}{4}$, $\frac{3}{4}$ and $\frac{4}{4}$ times, and using minim beats, as in $\frac{2}{2}$, $\frac{3}{2}$ and $\frac{4}{2}$.

Music may also be written down using **quaver beats**. The other name for a quaver is an eighth note, so a time signature using 3 quaver beats is shown by $\frac{3}{8}$. This is the time signature you will meet most often which uses quaver beats. $\frac{3}{8}$ is described as **simple triple** time.

On page 30 we saw how *'Happy Birthday'* could be written in $\frac{3}{4}$ and $\frac{3}{2}$. Now we can write it yet another way - in $\frac{3}{8}$ time.

The beats are measured in ♩'s

The beats are measured in ♪'s

The beats are measured in ♪'s

The tune <u>sounds</u> the same but the composer <u>chooses</u> how he wishes to write it.

■ A whole bar of shorter notes may be joined (beamed) in $\frac{3}{8}$ time, but a separate beat still needs a separate rest. For example:

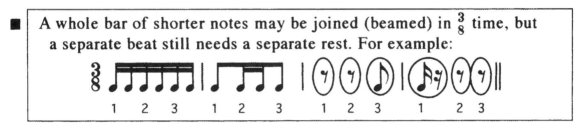

Exercise 69 Add bar lines to the following pieces in $\frac{3}{8}$ time.

Clementi. Sonatina Op.36

a)

J.S. Bach   Partita No.2

b)

Tchaikovsky. Op.19 No.2

c)

Scarlatti

d)

Saint Saens. The Carnival of the Animals

e)

| MORE EXERCISES with TIME SIGNATURES |

Exercise 70 Add the time signature to each of the following.

RE- WRITING in DIFFERENT TIME SIGNATURES

Exercise 71 Re-write each of these melodies using the different time signature indicated. Check to see that all shorter notes are correctly grouped (beamed) in the new time. The beginning of the first exercise has already been done as a guide.

● You already know some of the notes on the ledger lines and spaces above and below the bass stave. Now another note is added - C, written on the second ledger line below the stave.

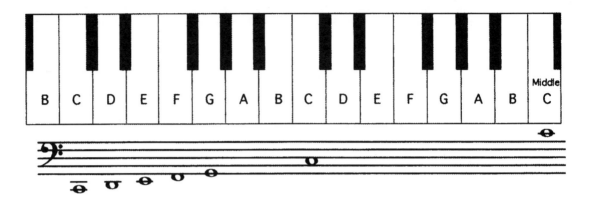

Exercise 72 Practise drawing these notes by copying out this tune onto the stave below. Do you recognise the tune?

Exercise 73 On the bass stave you now have three C's, three D's and three E's, all at different pitches. Can you draw them?

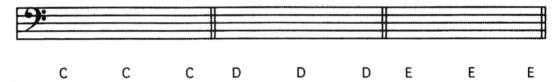

C   C   C   D   D   D   E   E   E

Exercise 74 This is a mixture of treble and bass ledger lines and spaces for you to name, Don't forget to add the word or sign for the accidental.

SINGING with SOLFA 7 : s, l, t, d r m f s

● In this group of tunes *l,* and *t,* below *do* are added.

Exercise 75 Sing each of these tunes with solfa names. Tap a steady beat or make hand signs as you sing.

Exercise 76 Compose the last two bars to finish each tune. Sing the completed tune.

REVISION EXERCISES : MAJOR and MINOR SCALES

Exercise 77 Add clefs, key signatures and accidentals, where needed, to make these scales. In minor scales, the harmonic or melodic minor form may be used. Mark the semitones. Write the tonic triad in the bar after each scale.

Bb major

a)

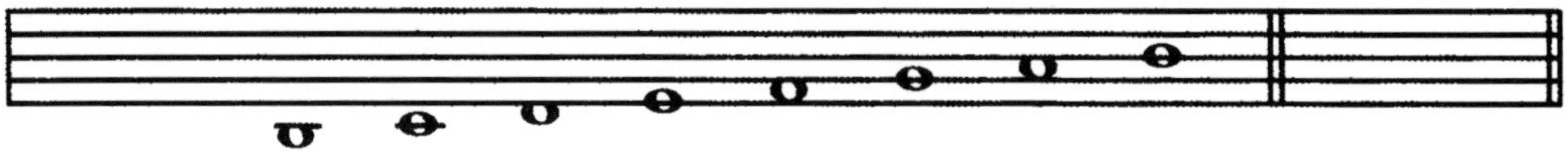

E minor

b)

D major

c)

E minor

d)

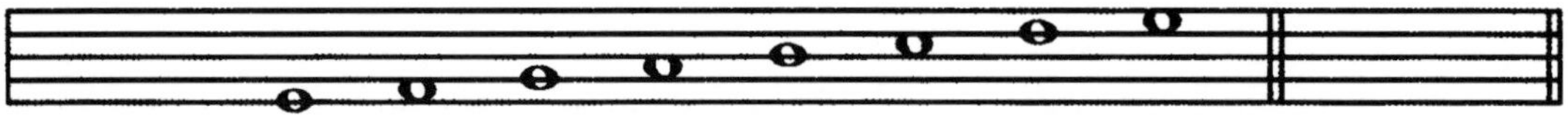

G major

e)

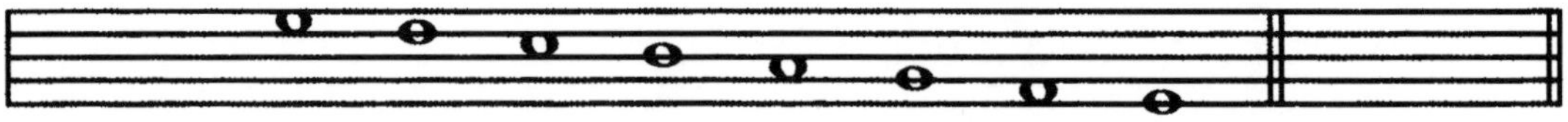

D minor

f)

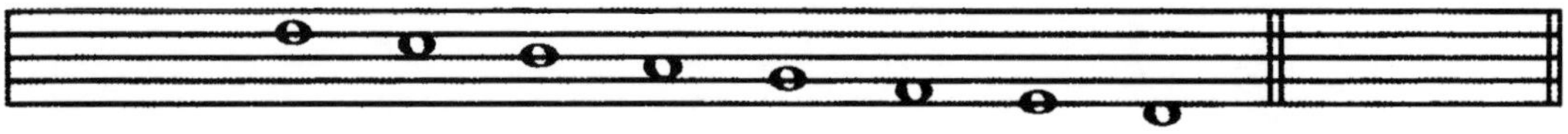

C major

g)

D minor

h)

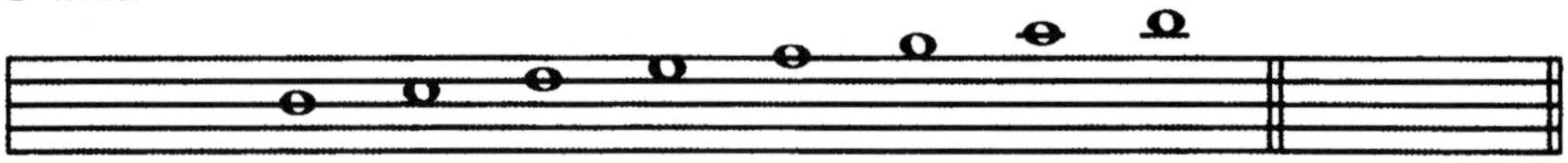

F major

i)

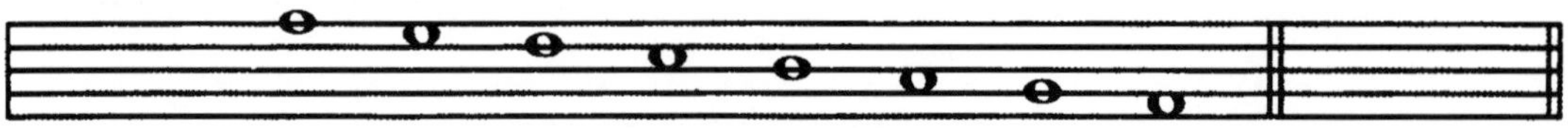

59

This piece is part of a Passepied by J.S.Bach. A 'passepied' is a kind of dance.
Study the music. Then answer the questions below.

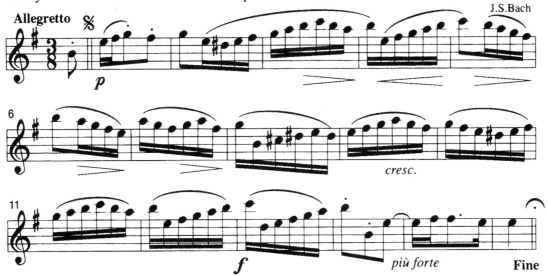

1. Explain these terms and signs. If necessary, refer to the glossary of terms on page 61.

   *cresc.*_____ **Fine**_____

   Allegretto _____ 𝄋 _____

   più forte _____ 𝄐 _____

2.a) Name the minor key in which the music is written. _____

   b) The raised 7th accidental (*si*) appears three times. Circle it each time it is written.

   c) Name the major key which shares this key signature. _____

   d) Give the letter name of the highest note in this extract. _____

   e) Look at bar 5 and then at bar 6.

       i) What do you notice about the rhythm? _____

       ii) What do you notice about the pitch? _____

3.a) Is $\frac{3}{8}$ time duple, triple or quadruple? _____

   b) Are the beats in $\frac{3}{8}$ time quavers, crotchets or minims? _____

   c) This is the beginning of the extract written in different time signatures. Complete
      these time signatures. Then write bar 3 according to the time signature you decided.

59

TEST 5

Q. 1   Add the missing barlines to the following melodies.

Johann Khün, 1638

Mahler: Symphony No.4

Q. 2   Re-write the following rhythm correctly grouped in $\frac{2}{2}$ time and complete the last bar by adding a rest at the place marked * .

Q. 3   Re-write this melody using the different time signature but without changing the effect.

Handel: Suite No. X

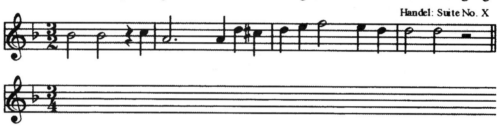

Q. 4 a)   Name 2 scales, a major and a minor,   Major_____   Minor_____
          which have a key signature of one flat.

     b)   Write one octave going up of this minor scale. Mark the semitones and add solfa names.
          Tick a box to show whether you have written the harmonic or melodic minor scale.

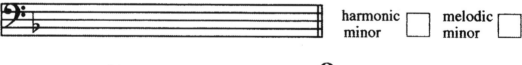

harmonic ☐ melodic ☐
minor   minor

Q. 5 Name these notes.

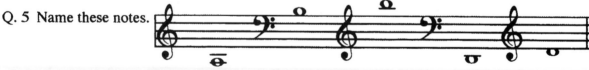

Q. 6 Answer the questions about the following melody.

Andante espressivo   Chopin. Nocturne Op.72

p dolce

a) Is the melody in G major or E minor? _____

b) What is the letter name of the first note? _____

c) Draw a circle around a note which is one octave lower than the first note.

d) Add the missing rests at * in bar 4.

e) Explain : Andante _____

     espressivo _____ dolce _____

GLOSSARY of MUSICAL TERMS

Terms and signs not previously introduced in the text are marked ●.

■ Tempo and Changes of Tempo

a tempo	back to normal speed	● Lento	slow
accelerando	gradually getting faster	● meno mosso	less movement , slower
Adagio	slow	Moderato	moderate speed
● Alla marcia	in the style of a march	M.M. ♩ = 60	60 crotchet beats in a minute
Allegretto	fairly quick and lively	● più mosso	more movement, faster
Allegro	quick and lively	poco rall. (rit.)	a little slower
Andante	walking speed	● Presto	fast
● con moto	with movement	rit. ritard. (rit.)	gradually getting slower
Largo	slow	● Vivace	lively
● Larghetto	fairly slow		

■ Dynamics

f **forte**	loud	*p* **piano**	soft
ff **fortissimo**	very loud	*pp* **pianissimo**	very soft
mf **mezzo forte**	moderately loud	*mp* **mezzo piano**	moderately soft
● *sf*	emphasised	● *fp*	loud, then soft at once
● *sempre f*	always loud	● *sempre p*	always soft
◁ cresc.	gradually getting louder	▷ dim. decresc.	gradually getting softer

■ Articulation

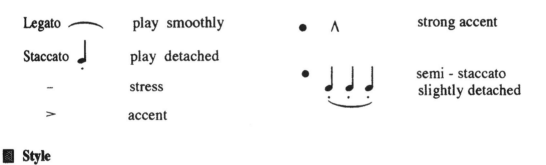

Legato	play smoothly
Staccato	play detached
–	stress
>	accent
∧	strong accent
	semi - staccato slightly detached

■ Style

dolce	sweetly	● *giocoso*	playful, merry
grazioso	gracefully	● *maestoso*	majestic
cantabile	singing style	● *espressivo*	expressive

■ Signs

⌢	pause
8va - - - - - -	Play one octave higher
8vb - - - - - -	Play one octave lower
:‖	Repeat
:‖:	Repeat the sections before and after
¹ | ²	On 1st playing, play bar 1 Play bar 2 after the repeat

● ℘ed. _____	Press the right pedal on the piano and release at _____
● ℘ed. ✳	or *
● **Fine**	End of piece

Other repeat directions

● D.C. Da Capo	repeat from the beginning
● D.S. Dal Segno	repeat from the sign 𝄋
● D.S. al Fine	repeat from the sign to the end
● 𝄋	See D.S. above

SOLFA HAND SIGNS

Ti (*t*)

La (*l*)

So (*s*)

Fa (*f*)

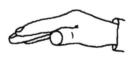

Mi (*m*)

Re (*r*)

Do (*d*)

HOMEWORK RECORD

DATE	WRITTEN EXERCISE Exercise number	CLAPPING / SINGING EXERCISE Exercise number	TEACHER COMMENT